9/92

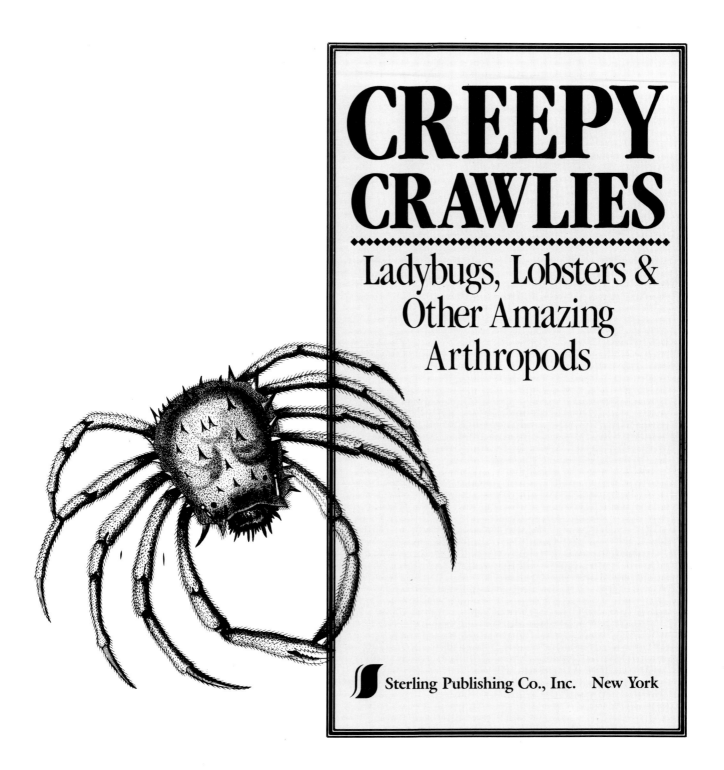

CREEPY CRAWLIES

Ladybugs, Lobsters & Other Amazing Arthropods

Sterling Publishing Co., Inc.   New York

Library of Congress Cataloging-in-Publication Data

Creepy Crawlies : ladybugs, lobsters & other amazing Arthropods.
     p.   cm.
   Includes Index.
   Summary: Discusses the evolution of arthropods, their characteristics,
their adaptability to many habitats and environments, and their relationship
to humans.
   ISBN 0-8069-8336-1
   1. Arthropoda—Juvenile literature.   2. Adaptation (Biology)—Juvenile
literature. [1. Arthropods. 2. Adaptation (Biology)]   I. Sterling
Publishing Company.
QL434.15.C74   1991
595′.2—dc20
                                           90-27531
                                              CIP
                                              AC

10 9 8 7 6 5 4 3 2 1

Published in the United States in 1991 by
Sterling Publishing Company, Inc.
387 Park Avenue South, New York, N.Y. 10016
Published in Great Britain by Natural History
Museum Publications under the title
Ladybirds & Lobsters / Scorpions and Centipedes . . .:
Introducing the Arthropods
© 1991 British Museum (Natural History)
Distributed in Canada by Sterling Publishing
% Canadian Manda Group, P.O. Box 920, Station U
Toronto, Ontario, Canada M8Z 5P9
Printed and bound in Hong Kong
All rights reserved

Sterling ISBN 0-8069-8336-1

Contents

Preface

The arthropod group contains animals as diverse as ladybugs, lobsters, scorpions and centipedes. Although these animals may seem to be very different from each other, they all have two striking things in common: their limbs have joints and their skeletons are on the outside of the body.

This book looks at a vast range of arthropods and highlights their versatility. By examining the ways in which they are adapted to survive in a wide range of frequently hostile environments, the book helps explain the enormous success of arthropods.

It describes, among other things, their colorful bodies, which help to fool prey and predators, and the complex structures that some build as communal homes.

Arthropods inevitably come into contact with humans. The book examines our relationships with arthropods, from harmless house spiders to the mosquitoes that transmit malaria and the locusts that destroy our crops.

The origins of the group are also considered. Fossils help reveal the ways arthropods have evolved and adapted to new environments over millions of years.

This book was produced with the help of many people. I would like to thank the writers, scientists and designers who have contributed to this project.

NEIL CHALMERS Director
The Natural History Museum
1991

5

Chapter 1
Introducing arthropods

What is an arthropod?

The term *arthropod*, meaning "jointed limb", was first coined over 140 years ago. Today it is used to desribe a very large group of animals found all over the world.

How many kinds are there?

So far, around 1.3 million different kinds of arthropods have been found, but there are certainly a lot more species to be discovered. Some scientists believe there may be as many as 30 million altogether.

7

How long have arthropods existed?

Arthropods have a spectacularly long history and were around long before most of the better known animal groups. The earliest known arthropods have been found in rocks over 600 million years old. At that time all arthropods were marine, but gradually land-living forms evolved. By 300 million years ago one group, the insects, had taken to the air and enormous dragonflies darted around the primeval forests. Today, insects are the largest and most diverse arthropod group and still the only one able to fly.

The giant dragonfly had a wingspan of up to 32 inches.

What makes an animal an arthropod?

All arthropods have certain characteristics in common. They have jointed limbs which nearly always occur in pairs. These can vary in number from three pairs in most insects to over 350 pairs in some millipedes.

Probably the most important single characteristic common to virtually all arthropods is their hard outer skeleton, called an exoskeleton. In most arthropods the exoskeleton incorporates material called chitin. Depending on the balance of its constituents, the exoskeleton may be rigid or flexible, waterproof or permeable.

One disadvantage of an exoskeleton is that it will not expand. To grow, arthropods must shed their old skeleton for a new one which, before it hardens, is sufficiently flexible to allow some expansion.

Having a tough skeleton outside the body does, however, have many advantages. In land-living arthropods the waterproof exoskeleton protects them from the moisture-sapping rays of the sun. This factor, more than any other, has enabled arthropods to colonize every terrestrial habitat, including some of the world's hottest and driest places.

But their success has not been limited to the land. In the sea, where being watertight is important for maintaining the correct concentration of body fluids, crustaceans are the dominant group. Arthropods, such as krill and microscopic copepods, occur in enormous numbers and form the basis of many important marine food chains.

Arthropods are important for our survival. On land, their activities as pollinators provide us with many plant products, including fruits, and some marine arthropods are a direct food source. But they are also our competitors for the Earth's resources – undoubtedly we have a constant battle trying to prevent them from consuming our food crops. Their ability to colonize so many different environments, to adapt rapidly to changes in their habitats and to utilize a wide range of substances for food has made arthropods the most successful and diverse animals on Earth.

Arthropods are usually divided into four main groups . . .

Water flea

Velvet swimming crab

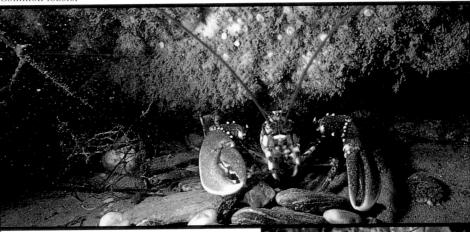

Crustaceans – crabs and their relatives

Crustaceans, which include some of the largest arthropods known, are predominantly aquatic and occur throughout the world in both marine and freshwater environments. They vary greatly in size – some water fleas are only one hundredth of an inch long while the largest crabs have a body width of 12 inches and a leg span of some 10 feet.

Red coral shrimp

Woodlouse

Edible crab

Desert millipede

Myriapods – centipedes and millipedes

Myriapods fall into two distinct groups, the centipedes (Chilopoda) and millipedes (Diplopoda).

There are about 1800 species of centipedes. Most of them are active predators with poisonous fangs. They vary in length from one-eighth of an inch to more than eight inches.

Millipedes species number about 7000, all of which are vegetarian, feeding mainly on decaying plant material. The smallest species are only a fraction of an inch in length, the longest up to a foot.

Stone centipede

Soil mites

Harvestman spider

Woodlouse spider

Arachnids –
spiders and their relatives

Spiders, scorpions, mites, ticks and eight other smaller groups make up the arachnids. All members of the group, with the exception of some mites, have four pairs of legs. Both spiders and scorpions are predatory and often poisonous. Altogether there are some 75,000 species of arachnids of which about half are spiders.

Desert scorpion

Imperial scorpion

Lace-web spider

Lesser stag beetle

Insects

For sheer numbers and diversity, insects are unsurpassed by any other animal group. Around 1.1 million species are known and there are probably millions more awaiting discovery. Insects are characterized by having three distinct body parts (head, thorax and abdomen), three pairs of legs and usually two pairs of wings.

With the exception of the sea, practically every type of environment can support insect life.

Peacock caterpillars

14

Common earwig

Lacewing

Holly blue butterfly

Burying beetle

Back chafer

ing mantis

Common wasp

Blue Mormon butterfly

15

Chapter 2

How arthropods grow

All arthropods live within the confines
of a rigid exoskeleton. Although the
inner organs expand as arthropods
mature, the outer skeleton remains fixed
in size and shape.

**How then do arthropods manage to
grow?**

If you lived inside a suit of armor, you too would have to shed it to grow!

To increase in size, an arthropod has to discard its tight-fitting cuticle, and replace it with a more spacious new one. This process is called molting.

Molting

At a certain time, hormones in an arthropod's body begin to act upon its outer covering, which soon becomes thin and weak. Often after a period of vigorous activity the brittle cuticle becomes loosened and finally splits. Underneath, a new skeleton has been forming. Now the arthropod pulls itself free of the old dried-out skeleton to reveal the fresh one below. At first the new cuticle is soft, pale and limp, but soon it expands, hardens and becomes colored, giving the arthropod a new protective coating.

Centipedes, millipedes, crustaceans and some arachnids molt at certain intervals throughout their lives. In contrast, most insects molt only during the early part of their lives, reaching sexual maturity with their last molt.

Some arthropod larvae look like perfect miniatures of their parents – they simply increase in size as they molt and grow. Others differ from the adults in almost every respect – they change dramatically as they grow.

The development of insects

As insects grow, most undergo an incredible transformation – there is often no resemblance at all between the larvae and the adult insects.

This transformation is illustrated by the mayfly and its larva.

Would you have guessed that these two creatures were both phases in the life of a mayfly?

Mayfly larvae (or nymphs) resemble shrimps. They live underwater in ponds or rivers and eat algae and decaying plant material. Some kinds molt more than 20 times while in their aquatic environment. At a particular time of year when they have reached a certain stage of growth, they rise to the surface and molt to reveal the penultimate stage in their lives. Although these winged creatures resemble adults, their legs are not fully developed. They fly off to find a sheltered place, and molt for the last time, revealing the mature adults.

Another example of diversity in a life cycle is the nymphalid butterfly and its larva.

The larvae of these butterflies (caterpillars) finally reach their full size after months or even years of almost

nonstop eating. Then they begin to prepare themselves for the final stage in their development. They spin silk pads to attach themselves securely to twigs or plant stems. In this suspended state their bodies begin to change. (The transitional form is known as the pupa.) When the transformation is complete the winged adult emerges.

Why do many insects go through these amazingly different forms as they grow? Why don't they emerge from the egg as tiny winged insects?

One reason is that in insects, larval and adults stages fulfill very specific functions. The prime function of larvae is to eat to provide the energy for growth. The main function of the adult is to reproduce. An extreme example of this is the adult mayfly which may live only for a day – just long enough to find a mate and for the female to lay her eggs!

Another reason is that by having different habitats and food sources, insect larvae and adults do not compete with each other.

A coxcomb prominent caterpillar eats its recently shed skin

Although they are superb eating machines with large efficient jaws, many insect larvae are poorly adapted for other tasks:

● they cannot mate since their sexual organs are undeveloped;

● they are slow, clumsy movers since their legs are rudimentary and they have no wings;

● they cannot withstand attacks since they are covered only by a fairly thin cuticle. (The really hard exoskeleton develops only in the adult after the last molt.)

Because they are physically vulnerable, larvae are often camouflaged to evade predators; or they may have bright warning colors to show that they are poisonous to eat. (You can find out more about arthropod colors in chapter 5.)

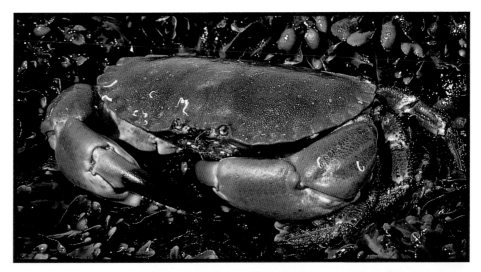

The development of crustaceans

Freshwater and marine crustaceans develop differently. Freshwater crustaceans tend to follow a direct line of development – the young being small replicas of the adults. Marine crustaceans, on the other hand, go through dramatic changes as they grow.

It is likely that, as for insects, the development paths were originally determined partly by the availability of food. The sea has a variety of food sources, and marine crustaceans may have evolved so that the larvae fed on a different food source from the adults.

A good example of this among marine crustaceans is the edible crab.

The adult edible crab and its larval form are about as different as you could imagine.

The adult lives among rocks and crevices in coastal waters. It is carnivorous and feeds on mussels, breaking open their shells with its powerful pincers. In contrast, the comma-shaped early larval stage floats freely in the water. It catches prey by lashing its forked tail through swarms of plankton, some of which becomes trapped between the tail forks and the larva's shell. The food is then maneuvred toward the larva's mouth.

Adult barnacles bear little resemblance to their larvae. Adults spend their lives glued to rocks or the bottoms of boats. Early planktonic larval stages float freely while more developed ones crawl about on the seabed. Using their feathery limbs, the adults filter the water for plankton of almost any shape or size, while the larvae use their hairy antennae to sweep the water for smaller planktonic plants. Clumps of these plants caught on the larva's sharp hairs are fed back through the mouthparts.

Freshwater crustaceans have adapted to an environment which has a limited range of available food. Both adults and young exploit the same food source.

The adult and larval forms of the freshwater crayfish resemble each other quite closely. Both are found in clean lowland rivers and feed by scavenging.

The development of myriapods

Millipedes

Rather than simply expanding in size, millipedes grow by adding groups of three or more segments after each molt.

Centipedes

Centipedes can be divided into two groups according to the way they develop - one group hatches from the egg with a full complement of legs, (left) while the other hatches with seven pairs of legs or fewer and adds segments and legs in the early stages of development (right).

The development of arachnids

Young spiders (spiderlings) closely resemble their parents. Each time they molt they grow larger and become more highly developed.

An interesting example of molting is found among tarantulas. They stop feeding and withdraw into retreats to molt. There they lie on their backs and the lengthy process begins.

The young tarantula shown below lacks the density of color and hair of the adult (inset). Since they are likely to fall prey to other spiders – even their own parents – spiderlings have to become independent as soon as possible

A wolf spider carrying young on her back

Garden spider spiderlings emerging from their nest

Chapter 3
All the colors of the rainbow

Many of the most striking colors of the natural world are found among arthropods. Butterflies, ladybirds and caterpillars are familiar colored arthropods, but there are many more exotic ones, such as gold bugs and red land crabs.

red – Eleven-spotted ladybirds   orange – Monarch butterfly

yellow – Longhorn beetle

purple – Locust

en – Golden chafer bug

blue – Lycaenid butterfly

How are these spectacular colors produced?

Arthropod colors are produced in three different ways

Light is composed of a whole spectrum of colors. When it falls on an object some colors are absorbed and others reflected. This crab is red because pigments in its body absorb all the colors of the spectrum except red, which they reflect. This phenomenon is known as chemical color.

Many butterflies owe their iridescence to light playing on the scales of their wings. Although the scales themselves are unpigmented, they produce intense shimmering color when light falls upon them. This is known as structural color since it is caused by an interaction between light and thin layers that make up the scales. Which colors are reflected depends on the thickness of the layers and the gap between them, as well as the angle at which the light hits the layers. Because these vary over butterflies' wings, the wings appear multicolored. The effect is the same as when light falls on an oily puddle and thin films of oil reflect colors.

Glowing colors

Arthropods such as glow worms, do not need an outside source of light to glow. They glow as a result of the reactions of chemicals in their bodies, which produce light. This phenomenon is known as bioluminescence.

'd wing butterfly specimen, photographed from a
tly different angle, shows the effect of structural color.

Uses of color

Bait

These blue lights photographed in a New Zealand cave are glowing fungus gnat larvae. Flying insects lured by their bright glow are snared in sticky threads trailing from the larvae. The larvae haul in the threads and devour their victims.

Warning and display

The startlingly vivid colors of some arthropods help to frighten off predators, or to attract attention away from vulnerable body parts.

A peacock butterfly flashes 'eyes' on its wings at predatory birds.

Clashing stripes of red, yellow and black warn predators that arthropods can retaliate by stinging or biting, or that they taste unpleasant.

Common wasp

Monarch caterpillar

Blind sequoia millipedes glow with a greenish light, warning predators of their bitter taste.

Jester bug

Sex

Arthropods use different types of color as sexual signals. In many species, males and females are colored differently. These differences help arthropods to distinguish possible mates. Sometimes the colors are visible to arthropods but not to us – we have to use ultraviolet light to see them.

Camouflage

Blending in with the surroundings can often help to deceive predators. Many arthropods have evolved effective and frequently bizarre forms of camouflage.

Small White butterfly under ultra-violet light

Small White butterfly under normal light

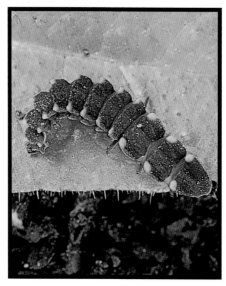

Glow worms (which are actually beetles) are probably the most famous glowing arthropods. The glow is used to attract mates. At night the wingless females turn their glowing abdomens up to the sky to attract males flying overhead. The males have a subdued glow, perhaps to warn off other males.

The peppered moth is a well-known example of the way color has influenced the survival of a species. During the nineteenth century the numbers of dark brown peppered moths increased while the lighter variety became less common.

Sargassum crab

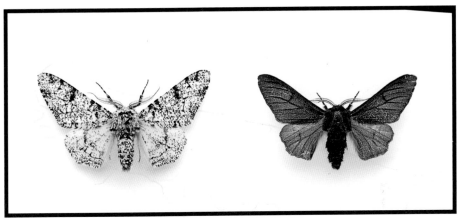

This happened because the dark moths were better adapted to life in the increasingly grimy environment of industrial England – they merged in with their dark surroundings.

As drillers for sap, shieldbugs spend their time exposed on the surface of trees, vulnerable to attack from birds and other predators. Effective camouflage is their first line of defence.

Some species of caterpillar have shading on their bodies that makes them look flat so that predators, looking for solid prey, fail to pick them out from their background.

Several species of spiders live on the bark of trees; blending into their background is essential for them as they lie in wait for prey.

An Australian lichen spider has tufts of Hair on its legs which match lichen-covered bark.

Many jumping spiders hunt against a background of tree bark. They are often superbly camouflaged.

Jumping spider on the prowl

Mimicry

Other arthropods are even more skillful in the art of camouflage – rather than simply being the same color as their background, they actually mimic some aspect of it.

Merveille du jour

Some arthropods that live on trees or plants evade their predators by resembling fresh bird droppings!

A female praying mantis guards a brood of youngsters. The mother resembles the stem of the thorn bush on which she sits while her offspring mimic the actual thorns.

Since leaves are common in terrestrial habitats it is not surprising that many insects have come to look like them.

While resembling a leaf in shape, the body of this bush cricket (from Trinidad) also incorporates features of a dead or dying leaf. The cricket even copies symptoms of fungal attack and the blotch mines caused by leaf-mining moths.

Resting on a leaf in a Malaysian rain forest, a bush cricket not only matches the color of its surroundings perfectly but also includes leaf veins and disease blotches to enhance the deception.

Some arthropods use deception to evade their predators. Although they resemble dangerous arthropods, they themselves are harmless. Their warning colors prevent them from being eaten.

Many wasps are capable of inflicting a painful sting. By looking like a wasp, a harmless hover fly deters its predators.

Mutillid wasps (also called velvet ants), have the most painful sting of all insects — not surprisingly they are frequently mimicked.

Some ground beetles are such good wasp mimics that scientists can identify precisely which species of mutillid the beetle is mimicking.

Many spiders also mimic mutillid wasps. This jumping spider resembles several species of Malaysian mutillids.

Its abdomen (on the left) looks like the wasp's head while the spider's head is on the right.

Chapter 4
Battling for survival

The range of arthropod weapons

In general, adult arthropods are well equipped for battle. A scorpion, for example, has jagged jaws, powerful pincers and a poisonous sting in addition to its thick, protective exoskeleton.

Claws and jaws

Many other arthropods have similarly effective weapons. Crabs and lobsters have pincers which, in a few species, are strong enough to remove a human finger.

European lobsters live in offshore waters. To escape predators they often retreat, tail first, into a crevice. Powerful pincers then confront the attacker.

Unlike most crabs, robber crabs live almost entirely on land. Their powerful claws can break into the coconuts which they eat.

Poisons

Another very effective weapon in both attack and defense is a poisonous sting. Scorpions are well known for their stings, but although all species are poisonous, most are not deadly to humans.

Many spiders also use poison to subdue or kill prey, but only a few species are deadly to humans. Probably the best known is the black widow spider.

Although this North American species is small, less than one and one-fifth inch across, the female's poisonous bite may be deadly if untreated.

Another extremely poisonous spider is the Sydney funnel web. Funnel web spiders belong to a group which includes bird-eating spiders or tarantulas. Most of this group are burrowers and the Sydney funnel web is no exception. Its burrow has a silken funnel at the entrance from which the spider gets its name.

Catching their prey

Most carnivorous arthropods have to hunt down or trap their food. To do this they have evolved highly ingenious methods of capture.

Sticky spider's webs are superb traps for flying insects.

Bolas spiders capture their victims with a sticky ball which they swing from a line. They then pull the ball, with prey attached, back up to the lair . . .

Trapdoor spiders rely on surprising their prey. The spider digs a burrow and covers it with a silken lid. Then, leaving the lid fractionally open, it lurks at the top of the burrow.

If a suitable animal strays near the lid the spider lunges out and bites it with its poisonous fangs. The prey is then dragged down into the burrow and consumed.

Dragonfly nymphs also take their prey by surprise. They conceal themselves in vegetation or mud on stream beds and lie in wait. When a small fish or tadpole approaches, the nymph shoots out its extendible jaws to grab the prey.

This strange creature is a caprellid, a marine crustacean which catches its prey in the same way as the praying mantis. It perches, unseen, on fronds of seaweed, waiting to grasp unsuspecting prey between its powerful pincers.

Virtually invisible against a background of plant leaves, the praying mantis waits for prey to wander within its reach. With its powerful forelegs folded in front as though praying, it is poised to pounce.

The mantis eats its prey alive.

Ant lion larvae (the immature stage of a dragonfly-like insect) ambush their prey. After digging a conical pit the ant lion larva lies buried at the bottom, with only its enormous jaws protruding, waiting for its victims.

When an ant scurries over the edge of the pit, the ant lion larva is alerted and flicks sand to knock the ant down into the bottom of the pit.

Then it seizes the ant between its large powerful jaws and begins to eat.

With their numerous long legs, centipedes are well adapted for high-speed hunting. Voracious carnivores, they feed on worms, snails and other arthropods, or even on lizards, toads and mice in the case of the

Tiger beetles have long legs for rapid pursuit and enormous biting jaws with which they can crush even the hardest outer skeleton. They will eat any animal small enough to fit between their jaws.

Speed and strength rather than stealth and cunning help some arthropods to catch their prey. Many have long legs and greatly enlarged, sometimes poisonous jaws which make them efficient hunters and killers.

largest tropical centipedes. They kill
their prey and paralyse with a bite
from their poisonous fangs.

Mantis shrimps, like the land-living
praying mantis, have powerful
forelegs and use the element of
surprise to catch their prey. They
have evolved into two distinct types
depending on the food they eat –
some have spiny forelegs on which
they spear small fishes, while others
have powerful forelegs to smash the
shells of prey such as snails and
crabs.

The action of the 'spearer' when
catching its prey is one of the fastest
animal movements known – taking less
than eight-thousandths of a second.

A 'smasher' can deliver a blow with a
force matching that of a small caliber
bullet – enough to break out of a glass
tank.

Food supplies for arthropod young

Many wasps lay their eggs on top of a
living food source. Later their
developing larvae will consume it.

One example of this is the spider wasp.
The sting of this large wasp can paralyse
a spider three times its size.

It then drags the spider into a hole which
it has prepared and, after laying a single
egg on top of the spider, covers the hole.
When the wasp larva hatches it eats the
spider live.

Chapter 5
Food and feeding

How are arthropods able to thrive in so many different habitats? One reason for their success is that, as a group, they are able to exploit virtually any natural substance as a food source.

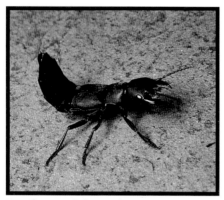

Devil's coach horse beetles eat
other insects and slugs

Book lice eat molds growing on paper

Tobacco beetles eat tobacco

Carpet beetles eat woollen carpets

**The range of
arthropod foods**

Leather beetles eat leather

. . . Some more attractive to humans than others!

Robber crabs eat coconuts

Locusts eat leaves

Lobsters eat fish

Mouthparts and limbs for the job

To consume this extraordinary range of foods, arthropods have evolved specially modified mouthparts and limbs. This may have happened to a much greater extent in arthropods than in other animals because their chitinous skeletons were more readily adaptable than internal bones.

House flies vomit digestive juices which reduce solid food to a sort of liquid soup. The liquefied food is then soaked up through the labellum - a sponge-like extension of the mouth.

Although mosquitoes are notorious blood suckers, it is only the female that requires this diet to ensure successful maturation of her eggs.

She is attracted to a host animal's skin by its moistness and warmth. Once settled, the mosquito injects an anticoagulant into the animal's

blood to prevent clotting and then sucks up the liquid meal through its syringe-like mouthparts.

Aphids feed on the sap of trees and plants, piercing the plant with sharp pointed mouthparts, called stylets. Pressure of the sap in the plant

carries it up the stylets and into the animal's gut.

Butterflies suck up nectar through their long tubular mouthparts, which are kept coiled up like a hose when not in use.

Strainers

By opening its feathery limbs like parasols an atyid prawn can filter plankton from fresh water. The food is then transferred by these limbs to the mouthparts.

Barnacles strain sea water for food with their modified net-like limbs.

The large claw of this fiddler crab is not used for feeding but for signalling to females and for the defense of its territory.

To feed, the crab uses its small pincer to carry minute particles of mud to its mouth where anything edible is strained out.

Raspers

Horseshoe crabs, protected by a domed shield, burrow their way through the top layer of sand or mud on the seabed. They use jaw-like extensions on the base of their walking legs to trap prey such as clams and worms. They grind up their meal with these 'rasping' limbs before they pass it forward to the mouth on the underside of their bodies. The limbs of many simple arthropods, such as those of the horseshoe crab, are often used for both movement and feeding.

Chapter 6
Master builders

The range of arthropod buildings

Many arthropods, particularly some insects, have evolved remarkably complex building skills and are able construct a wide variety of nests and shelters.

Garden spider

Leaf-cutter bee

Land crab

Mud dauber wasp

Weaver ant

Leaf-rolling cricket

Froghopper

Leaf-rolling beetle

Sand wasp

Building techniques and uses

To build such a great variety of structures, arthropods employ a number of different materials and techniques depending on the purpose of the structure.

The building of a sticky silk net to catch prey, particularly prey that flies, is common amongst spiders, but they are not the only arthropods to use silk nets.

The caddisfly larva, like many immature insects, is aquatic. It spins an elaborate funnel-shaped net and anchors it to aquatic plants or twigs. The running water of the stream in which it lives keeps the funnel open, and the net strains small organisms out of the water for the larva to eat at leisure.

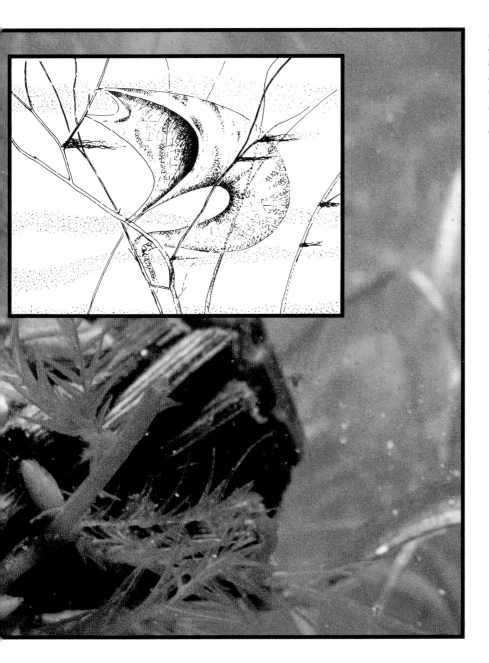

Apart from building traps, arthropods also build shelters. Some are permanently fixed in one place and may be communal dwellings. In other cases an individual may build a portable home which it carries around. Most caddisfly larvae do this. They build a silk cocoon and then decorate it with dead plant matter or particles of sand and gravel. Some species attach shells and tiny snails to the outside of the cocoon to camouflage its outline. The exact method of construction and materials used vary from species to species.

In general, larval stages are more vulnerable than the adult stage, so most arthropod structures are concerned with nest building and protection of the eggs or young. Many arthropods such as bees, leaf-cutter ants and leaf-roller crickets, make use of plant material to build nests. Others, such as digger and mud dauber wasps make use of materials such as sand, mud and clay to construct their nests. Some simply excavate a hole in the ground while others construct elaborate fortresses. Many of the social wasps build amazingly intricate communal nests using a mixture of wood shavings and saliva. The variety of materials and techniques seems to be endless.

Inside a hive

A honeybee comb is a marvel of engineering.

It consists of a series of carefully constructed hexagonal wax cells. If the cells were round or even octagonal or pentagonal, there would be empty spaces between them. This would not only be a waste of space but would necessitate the buiding of separate walls for all or part of each cell. These difficulties can be avoided by using triangles, squares or hexagons - but of the three the hexagon has the smallest circumference for its area and is therefore the most economical to use.

Apart from making the most of the space available, the way in which hexagons fit together gives the comb great strength. A comb measuring 15 by 9 inches and containing only 1½ ounces of wax can hold almost 4½ pounds of honey.

To begin building, bees gather together into a dense ball within which they maintain a temperature of 95°F – the temperature needed to produce wax. It is secreted from special glands in the bees' abdomens.

In a conventional hive, building begins at the top of a frame, usually at two or three different places at once. While the walls of the first cells are being constructed, new cells are started lower down the frame. Eventually they join to form the complete comb. The cell walls are built at a gradient of 13° to prevent honey from running out. Cell walls are only 3 thousandths of an inch thick with a margin of error of less than 8 millionths of an inch! Truly astounding precision.

Spiders' webs

Although all spiders can produce silk only some kinds spin it into webs. The silk they use (produced by special spinning glands in the spider's abdomen) is a remarkable material – it is twice as strong as steel, finer than human hair and can stretch to three times its own length. It is also edible, so before building a new web a spider may eat the old one and recycle virtually all the silk.

The typical spider's web, such as might be seen in a garden, is known as an orb web and consists of three major elements: frame threads which form the web's outline and serve as tethers; radial threads which converge into a central point; and the catching spiral. Only the catching spiral is sticky.

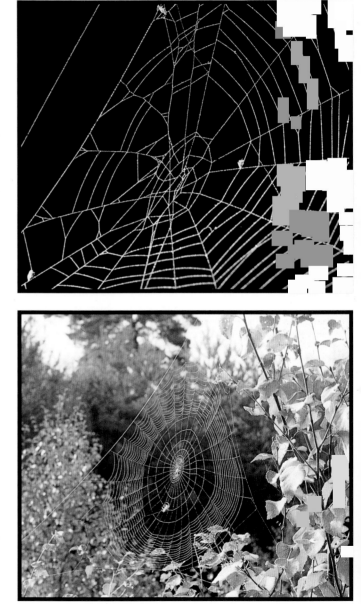

In the middle of the web is an area known as the hub. It consists of a concentration of strands, although in some webs the hub is missing completely and the web appears with a large hole in the center. Between the hub and the catching spiral is the free zone. This enables the spider to change quickly from one side of the web to the other depending on which side the prey has been snared.

With more than 2000 species of orb-web spiders there is great variation in web architecture. By using a minimum of material (less than .0000175 ounces of silk) and time (about an hour to build a typical web), spiders have an extremely efficient method of catching prey.

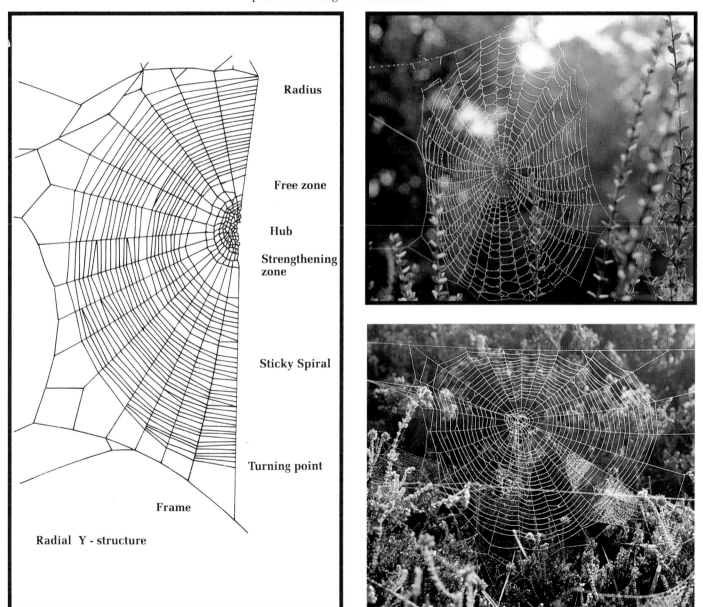

Radius

Free zone

Hub

Strengthening zone

Sticky Spiral

Turning point

Frame

Radial Y - structure

Termite towers

Perhaps the most spectacular examples of arthropod structures are termite mounds. There are more than 2000 species of termites, most of which live in tropical or semitropical regions. Unlike most insects, termites cannot withstand too dry an atmosphere.

Thriving in warmth and high humidity, they design complex nests to achieve these conditions.

Depending on the local climate, termite mounds come in a variety of shapes.

Some termites live in areas of very high rainfall, such as tropical forests. To protect themselves from the torrents, they build extraordinary roofs on their towers – making the structures look like a series of mushrooms stacked one on top of the other.

Compass termites live in the Australian outback. Their towers are up to 16½ feet long and 10 feet high but very narrow. Their short sides face exactly north-south so that the surface exposed to the rays of the midday sun is small, while the long sides catch the morning and evening sun. In the cold season, termites congregate on the east side in the morning and the west side in the evening in order to gain maximum heat from the sun.

The interior architecture of many termite mounds is even more impressive than the exterior. Chambers are laid out according to their different functions which may indicate a definite building plan. Inside some mounds there may be as many as two million individuals. Their oxygen consumption is considerable and without ventilation they would all suffocate within a day. It is only by an ingenious system of air conditioning that they avoid this fate.

The nest, which may be 6½ feet across, sits like a giant lollipop on a stick. Above it rises an empty hollow tower up to 10 feet high. When the nest gets too hot, worker termites rush to open a valve made of dried mud at the top. Hot, stale air escapes from the nest and rises up the tower. Near the top, the walls of the tower are so thin that the stale air, rich in carbon dioxide, seeps out while fresh air floods in. This cooler air sinks to the bottom of the tower and enters the nest from below. By opening and closing the valve in their nest the termites have complete control over the air flow through their underground environment.

Chapter 7
Taking up residence

Many arthropods are familiar to us because we come across them every day in our homes. Many kitchens contain thriving arthropod communities – beetles inhabit the woodwork, silverfish and wood lice live under the sink, ants forage the food cupboards, cockroaches lurk behind the stove and bluebottles buzz around the food.

Bedrooms have their own arthropod residents – people who sneeze when they get into bed should blame the dust mites that gather in the mattress. In some houses bed bugs swarm behind the wallpaper, coming out at night to feed on sleeping humans. Many other arthropods can be found throughout the home – perhaps the one we know best is the house spider, which patrols our rooms in search of a mate.

Bluebottle

Dust mite

Silverfish

Bed bug

For carnivorous arthropods, such as the house spider and the devil's coach horse beetle, our homes are an easy source of prey.

Some arthropods like to feed on our food. For bluebottles and houseflies, our wastebaskets are a gastronomic delight – rotting, oozing food attracts them because it is easy to turn into a solution which they can mop up with their sponge-like mouthparts.

Garden ants troop into the house in search of food which they can take back to their nests.

Why do these unwelcome visitors invade our homes?

Wasps build nests in the safety of the attic. This nest was started by a single queen. Now she lives there with 5000 of her offspring.

Clothes moths seek out our woolen fabrics to lay their eggs in. When the larvae hatch out, they munch their way through our clothes.

Parasitic arthropods, such as fleas, ticks and lice, are carried into our homes by us or our pets. Fleas, from our dogs and cats, lay a large number of eggs. Their larvae feed on detritus, especially flea droppings, and can reach maturity in less than a month.

Some arthropods are even specialized consumers of our household furnishings. For instance, the larvae of the carpet beetle slowly consume our woolen carpets; book lice feed on molds growing on paper and the glue holding our books together; and woodworms, the larvae of furniture beetles, tunnel around in our woodwork as they develop.

Carpet beetle

Furniture beetle

An arthropod in every bite!

Many arthropods find a congenial home amongst our food stores.

Larder beetles creep into our cupboards to find a suitable place to lay their eggs.

The newly hatched grubs gorge themselves on our supplies of bacon.

Cheese mites lay their eggs on cheese - this mature cheddar is infested with them

Spider beetles and their larvae are major pests of stored food. Apart from eating spices and sauce mixes, they feed on textiles and other apparently indigestible things.

Biscuit beetles infest our cookies, but, fortunately for chocolate lovers, tend to choose the dry crispy variety rather than chocolate-coated ones.

Open bags of flour can quickly become teeming with mites, caterpillars and beetle grubs.

Infestation – how can we stop it?

Some arthropods have benefited from modern improvements in housing, but many others have found them disastrous. Central heating, wall to wall carpeting and insulation have made our houses havens for heat seeking arthropods, such as pharaoh ants, but they have also threatened the damp habitats of woodlice, silverfish and spiders. The tiny clover mite, which molts and lays eggs in crevices in external brickwork, may wander into our homes but be thwarted by the high quality finish on our walls.

The once common bed bug is now rare in most developed countries.

Domestic pests have not all disappeared. Ants still invade our food cupboards, wasps and flies still buzz around our kitchens, and spiders still scurry across our floors.

Grain weevils

Clover mite

Woodlice

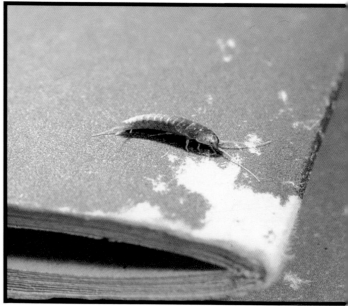

Silverfish

To prevent these pests from breeding in or near our homes our garbage cans should be kept covered. We should also watch out for ants' or wasps' nests near our houses. Often these are easy to find because there are a suspiciously large number of insects flying or crawling around near them.

Inside the house, food should be kept under cover – preferably in the refrigerator or in cupboards which can be tightly closed and which are well above floor level.

There are many insecticides available for killing insects and spiders. But these products are unpleasant to use, and although they may get rid of a few individual pests, they do not strike at the heart of an infestation. A better way to control pests is to keep them out in the first place.

Once inside the house, the bathroom is one of the most common sites for an encounter with a spider. How many times have you found a spider scrabbling around in your bath? Contrary to popular belief, these spiders do not climb up the drainpipe and through the plug hole only to find themselves trapped. In fact, they usually fall down the slippery sides of the bath. Recently, a device for rescuing spiders in this situation has come on the market. It consists of a small rope ladder which can be dangled down into the bottom of the bath, giving the spiders an easy escape route.

It is worth being kind to house spiders because they are completely harmless and they help to keep our homes free of more serious pests.

Chapter 8

Arthropods and humans

Disease carriers

Some arthropods pose a major threat
to human health, especially in the
hotter parts of the world. Many
tropical insects, mites and ticks feed
on human blood, and this is one of the
commonest ways in which some
serious diseases are spread.
Arthropods are particularly prevalent
in the tropics, so it is here that many
of the most debilitating human
diseases occur.

Anopheline mosquito feeding

Arthropods themselves are usually not the direct cause of diseases but, by feeding on man and other animals, they spread the microscopic organisms which produce the symptoms.

Arthropods which transmit diseases are known as vectors and different diseases have different vectors. For example, anopheline mosquitoes are the vectors for malaria and filariasis; black flies for river blindness; tsetse flies for sleeping sickness; body lice for typhus; fleas for plague; and certain kinds of ticks for

Lyme disease and some types of relapsing fever.

Of all the diseases carried by arthropod vectors, malaria is probably the most widespread. It has been estimated that, even today, there are at least two billion people at risk from malaria.

The main vector of malaria in Africa is the mosquito *Anopheles gambiae.*

Male mosquitoes do not feed on blood so only females carry the disease. To pass on the disease a mosquito must be infected with the malarial parasite, a

tiny single-celled organism called *Plasmodium.*

When an infected female *Anopheles* mosquito feeds on human blood, these organisms present in the mosquito's saliva, invariably get passed into the bloodstream. Their presence causes a raging fever – the sufferer alternates between feeling very hot and very cold with the fever returning every few days if not treated. In the worst forms of malaria sufferers may die.

River blindness today affects about 20 million people in Africa and central South America. The causative organism is a microscopic worm but the arthropod vectors responsible for transmission are various species of black flies

Since black flies breed in fast-flowing water, rivers and irrigation ditches are favourite sites for infestation. By feeding on human blood, black flies pass the worms into the bloodstream. They breed and spread to the skin and eyes. If untreated the disease can impair vision leading ultimately to total blindness.

Black fly

Another fly, the tsetse, carries a disease known as sleeping sickness. Like malaria and river blindness, the causative organism is microscopic and is passed to humans in the saliva of the fly when it takes a blood meal.

Sufferers from sleeping sickness become increasingly weak and tired as the disease takes hold. They eventually become too weak to eat and die.

Sleeping sickness currently affects 35 African countries and puts an estimated 36 million people at risk. However, the disease also affects cattle, and about a quarter of Africa, unable to sustain cattle for this reason, cannot be used to its full potential.

Tsetse fly feeding

Crop destroyers

Although arthropod vectors carry many serious diseases, it is not always humans and livestock that are under attack – arthropods can also be serious crop destroyers.

More than one-third of the world's crops are lost to arthropod pests. In Africa and Asia almost 50 percent of crops are lost in this way. Of all the arthropods, insects are the most voracious consumers of food crops.

Locusts are among the best known and most spectacular insect pests. Occurring mostly in Africa, these insects can congregate into massive swarms of many millions of individuals. These swarms may weigh hundreds of thousands of tons. Such a swarm can strip vast areas of greenery in a very short time.

Although few arthropod pests occur in such large numbers, many others also cause devastation. Here are some of the worst:

Brown planthopper – a major pest of rice in Asia

Nettle caterpillar – a major pest of coconut and oil palm in Southeast Asia

Aphid – a sap-sucking pest

Colorado beetle – the world's worst pest of potatoes

Armyworm – Africa's most notorious cereal pest

In fact, for any given crop there are dozens of arthropod pests – the problem remains how to control them.

Fighting back

Any attempt at effective control of arthropods, whether as disease carriers or crop destroyers, must take into account several factors. Most important is a detailed knowledge of the biology and ecology of the arthropod concerned, the animal or plant affected and, if relevant, the disease-causing organism involved.

Efforts to control vector-borne diseases have, not surprisingly, centered on control of the vector itself because without these intermediaries, diseases would not spread.

In the case of malaria, the insecticide DDT was used with some success in the 1940s, effectively eradicating malaria from southern USA and Europe. Parts of Africa and South America were also cleared of the disease. However, by 1950, two species of mosquito had already become immune to DDT. This, coupled with lack of funds, poor management and general complacency about the disease led to a resurgence of cases in areas formerly free of malaria. Nowadays more simple preventative methods which remove mosquito breeding sites are often preferred to nonspecific use of insecticide.

Modern pest control methods often try to combine cheapness with efficiency and environmental safety. Some success has been achieved in Zimbabwe using a very simple trap for tsetse flies.

Tsetse flies often feed on cows and are drawn to their shape and smell. Scientists researching tsetse fly behavior discovered that, after a cow shape, tsetse flies are most attracted to a square – especially a black one. Using this information some simple black, square traps were constructed with insecticide-impregnated netting attached. Scientists even managed to make the traps smell like cows. When the flies approached the trap they flew into the fine netting and were killed by the insecticide.

Unfortunately, not all pests can be controlled using simple traps. Sometimes an arthropod's life cycle is complex and the best way to stop the pest unclear. Most modern pest control methods used in the field rely on a combination of the best available techniques tailored for the particular pest concerned. Preventative measures which educate the local population are often the easiest way to begin fighting back.

Chapter 9
Ancient arthropods

The astonishing versatility of arthropods has contributed to the evolution of the huge variety of forms we find today. Like all living things, today's arthropods have evolved from earlier forms – those that could adapt to changes in their environment survived, while those that could not became extinct.

What do we know about these early arthropod forms and what can they tell us about the evolution of arthropods?

Bringing fossil arthropods back to life

We know that arthropods have been around for millions of years because portions of their bodies or traces of their activities, such as trails and burrows, have been found preserved in rocks up to 600 million years old. Apart from some worm-like animals, few other creatures are known to have existed at this time.

Some of these early arthropods were very different from those around today.

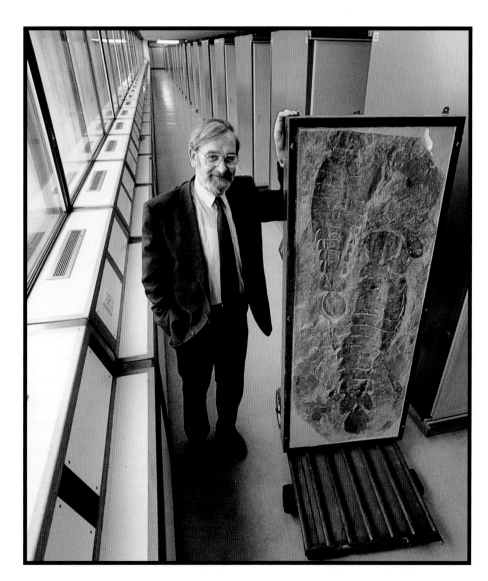

. . . This giant water scorpion was one of the largest arthropods that ever lived. The group died out 250 million years ago.

These old fossils, often distorted or broken, are the only evidence we have of such ancient creatures. But, using them, we can sometimes go back in time to reconstruct the lives of the early arthropods – to find out what they ate, how they moved, where they lived, and so on.

Judging by the fossils, some ancient arthropods would have looked almost identical to modern arthropods. Because their similar body parts were probably adapted to perform the same functions, it is likely that these early arthropods lived in much the same way as their modern relatives.

Ancient horseshoe crabs, and modern horseshoe crabs living 150 million years later, would probably be indistinguishable. Like their modern relatives, the first horseshoe crabs probably lived deep in the sea, emerging only in the spring at full moon and high tide to spawn on beaches.

Fossils are harder to interpret when there are no modern equivalents with which to compare them. In such cases it often helps to look at several fossils for clues as to how an animal lived.

This is the fossil of a trilobite, an ancient sea arthropod. The fossil shows its flattened body.

A second fossil shows a trilobite rolling up.

A third fossil shows a trilobite rolled up tighter.

A fourth fossil shows a trilobite in a tight ball.

Maybe trilobites rolled up into a ball when threatened – just as the pill millipede does today.

The incomplete history of arthropods

Collections of fossils of the same age may help us to investigate the life styles of the early arthropods, but they cannot explain how these creatures originated or what happened to them subsequently.

Which of the strange forms below were the ancestors of modern arthropods and which of them vanished, having failed to adapt to a changing Earth?

To answer these questions we would need to look at a series of fossils of different ages. Only then could we see how a particular arthropod had evolved over millions of years. In practice, however, this is rarely possible as most ancient arthropods vanished without trace.

Fossil survivors

The extent to which an animal is fossilized depends on where it dies and how tough its body parts are.

The best preservation occurs in mud, which, under compression, eventually hardens to stone. So,

usually, fossilized arthropods are ones that lived in or near water.

The great majority of fossils are of hard parts of an animal. So although many creatures may have been entombed in muddy sediment, few

became fossils because their body parts were too soft.

Large arthropods are preserved better than small ones. . .

. . . and fossils of the more durable body parts – such as wings – are often found without the rest of the body.

In some exceptional cases, it is possible to find fossils where even the softest parts are intact.

Fossil insects and spiders have been found exquisitely preserved in lumps of amber – the hardened resin of trees.

The Burgess Shale in Canada has been found to contain many fossils including arthropods which were exceptionally well preserved because they were caught in underwater mud slides and buried. Even the soft parts of animals which would normally have decayed and disappeared without trace have left impressions in the fine-grained shale.

Apart from giving us a glimpse of an ancient community, the Burgess Shale discovery has also helped to confirm the fact that many animals are *not* normally preserved as fossils.

Some of the animals found in the Burgess Shale are completely different from any living organisms, and may be the fossils of creatures that died out millions of years ago. Others may have been the precursors of modern forms, but without the discovery of intermediate stages we will never know for sure.

By 400 million years ago arthropods had left the sea and evolved into land-living creatures. Scorpions, mites and springtails – all adapted to surviving in damp areas – were some of the first land dwellers.

Great events in arthropod evolution

Six hundred million years ago, the first arthropods, believed to have evolved from a worm-like ancestor, lived in the sea. Today they are one of the most numerous and diverse of animal groups and are found in almost every part of the world.

What happened in between?

The fossil record, although incomplete, reveals some fascinating landmarks.

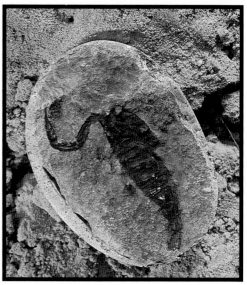

Insects, the first creatures to 'conquer' the air, appeared around 300 million years ago. Curiously, there are no fossils which show how wings developed – all the early fossils of insects have either well-developed wings or none at all.

Trilobites were once the most
common kind of arthropod. At their
most abundant, about 500 million
years ago, they had spread through
the seas and diversified into a great
number of species. Then, 250 million
years later, the group dwindled and
died out. No one knows why.

When flowering plants first evolved, about 100 million years ago, a huge range of new insect species developed. Some – such as butterflies and bees – began an intimate relationship with flowering plants through feeding and pollination. Insects soon became the dominant arthropod group on land and today 85 percent of all known animal species are insects.

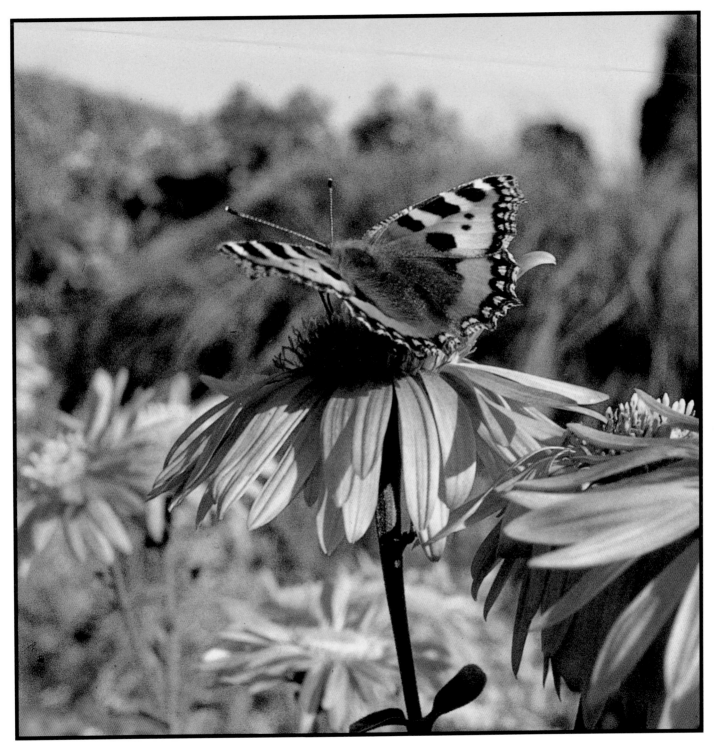

A last word

The modern arthropods featured in this book fall into four main groups:

Insects, which have three pairs of legs, wings, and one pair of antennae.

Arachnids, which have four pairs of legs and no antennae.

Crustaceans, which have two pairs of antennae (and almost all live in water).

Myriapods, which have bodies made up of many segments, each with one or two pairs of legs.

But there are some creatures that are difficult to place . . .

Velvet worms are soft animals with a caterpillar-like body. At first sight they seem unlikely to be related to arthropods, but the ancestors of insects and myriapods were probably similar.

'All-legs-and-no-body' sea spiders have four or more pairs of long jointed legs. Although they have a very different shape from arachnids, they may be related to them.

Water bears are tiny animals with four pairs of unjointed legs and a thin outer skeleton. Some scientists believe they are related to arachnids.

Because these creatures are alive today we can investigate them in much greater detail than fossils – not only can we study their general anatomy, but we can also probe into their cells to examine the genes that determine all their features.

This is one of the techniques scientists use to work out how different creatures are related – those with similar genes are more closely related than those with very different ones.

Such work can provide us with valuable clues about arthropod evolution. Every year some 12,000 new arthropod species are discovered. By studying these and continuing the search for new fossil arthropods, eventually we may be able to see how the 'primitive' ancient arthropods evolved into the most successful animal group on Earth.

ACKNOWLEDGEMENTS

H. Angel, Biofotos: acorn barnacle, 56; deathwatch beetle, 72.

D. Attenborough: horseshoe crab, 87.

J. & M. Bain, Natural History Photographic Agency: edible crab (adult), 23.

A. Bannister, Natural History Photographic Agency: velvet worm, 100; spider wasp, 49; tsetse fly, 79.

G. I. Bernard, Oxford Scientific Films: leather beetle, 52; cockroach, 68–69; larder or bacon beetle, 73.

C. Bett, Natural History Museum: desert scorpion, 13, 42–43.

S. Blackmore, Natural History Museum: robber crab, 44.

L. & T. Bomford, Ardea: crayfish (adult), 24.

G. Boxshall, Natural History Museum: barnacle (larva), 24.

J. Burton, Bruce Coleman: crayfish (juvenile), 24.

J. H. Carmichael, Natural History Photographic Agency: golden chafer beetle, 28; sargassum crab, 34–35.

N. Cattlin, Holt Studios: booklouse, 52.

H. Chaumeton, Natural History Photographic Agency: sea spider, 100.

G. Claridge, Natural History Photographic Agency: robber crab, 53.

J. Cooke, Oxford Scientific Films: desert millipede, 12; jumping spider, 37; Trinidad bush cricket, 39; trapdoor spider, 46; Opsiphanes butterfly, 55; garden spider, 58; mud dauber wasp, 58.

L. Crowhurst, Oxford Scientific Films: carpet beetle larva, 72.

S. Dalton, Natural History Photographic Agency: mayfly (adult), 20–21; hover fly, 46; desert locust, 53; bed bug, 69; cat flea, 71; spider beetle, 73.

G. du Fea, Planet Earth Pictures: leaf-cutter bee, 58.

J. Goode, Natural History Museum: blue mormon butterfly, 15; peacock caterpillars, 14.

P. Hillyard, Natural History Museum: giant centipede, 25; spirostrepid millipede, 25.

P. Hillyard & J. Martin, Natural History Museum: spider webs, 64–65.

R. Hoffman, Radford University, Virginia: sequoia millipede, 33.

J. D. Holloway, CAB International: nettle caterpillar, 81.

R. Hutchins, Mississippi Entomological Museum: leaf-rolling cricket, 59.

B. Ingle, Natural History Museum: edible crab, 23.

R. W. G. Jenkins, Natural History Photographic Agency: Sydney funnel-web spider, 45.

C. Jermy, Natural History Museum: garden spider spiderlings, 27.

R. & D. Keller, Natural History Photographic Agency: Australian lichen spider, 36–37.

R. Knightsbridge, Natural History Photographic Agency: Colorado potato beetle, 81.

Z. Leszczynski, Oxford Scientific Films: praying mantis, 47; lobster, 53.

K. Lewis, Oxford Scientific Films: robber flies, 40.

G. A. Maclean, Oxford Scientific Films: peacock butterfly, 33.

J. Martin, Natural History Museum: praying mantis, 15; nymphalid butterfly (life cycle), 20–21; lycaenid butterfly, 29; lycaenid caterpillar, 38.

S. Moore, Natural History Museum: imperial scorpion, 13.

G. Murrey, Jr., Oxford Scientific Films: bolas spider, 46.

Natural History Museum: peppered moth, 35; horseshoe crab, 57; atyid prawn, 56; garden ants, 70; biscuit beetle, 73; Burgess Shale fossils, 90

Natural History Photographic Agency: fungus gnats, 32.

Oxford Scientific Films: harvestman, 12–13; giant centipede, 12; giant centipede, 48; carpet beetle, 52.

P. Parks, Oxford Scientific Films: caprellid, 46–47; land crab, 58–59.

Prof. W. Peters: malaria parasite, 78–79.

L. Pitkin, Natural History Museum: common lobster, 11; red coral shrimp, 11; edible crab, 10; velvet swimming crab, 10–11; xanchid crab, 30; common lobster, 44.

L. Polunin, Natural History Photographic Agency: fiddler crab, 56.

G. Popov, Natural History Museum: desert locust (hoppers), 80; migratory locusts (mating), 80.

K. G. Preston-Mafham, Premaphotos: shieldbugs, 35; jumping spider, 37; praying mantis, 39; jumping spider, 41; ground beetle, 41; mutillid wasp 41; black widow spider, 45.

A. Romage, Oxford Scientific Films: leaf-rolling beetle, 59.

P. Sauer, Bruce Coleman: froghopper, 59.

P. Sharp, Oxford Scientific Films: pink-toed tarantula, 26–27.

J. Shaw, Natural History Photographic Agency: tiger beetle, 48.·

M. Simmonds, Birkbeck College, University of London: armyworm, 81.

K. Taylor, Bruce Coleman: glowworms, 31; sand wasp, 59.

D. Thompson, Oxford Scientific Films: pink-toed tarantula, 26–27.

M. Tweedie: coxcomb prominent caterpillar, 22; barnacle (adult), 24; molting centipede, 25; cave centipede, 25; wolf spider, 27; eleven-spot ladybirds, 28; jester bug, 33; glowworm (male), 34; glowworm (larva), 34; eyed hawk moth caterpillars, 36; alder moth caterpillar (early), 38; alder moth caterpillar (late), 38; merveille du jour moth, 38; bird dropping spider, 38; Malaysian bush cricket, 39; hover fly, 41; devil's coach horse beetle, 52; silverfish, 69; devil's coach horse beetle, 70; wood louse, 74; pill millipedes, 89.

S. von Eysinga-Meredith: black fly, 79.

M. Walker, Natural History Photographic Agency: water bear, 101.

P. Ward, Bruce Coleman: ant lion larva, 48; nest of tropical termites, 66.

A. Warren, Ardea: weaver ant, 59.

M. R. Wilson, Mississippi Entomological Museum: brown planthopper, 81.

All other photographs are from the Natural History Museum.

INDEX